PRESERVED STEAM

Geoff Swaine

AMBERLEY

Photographs by the author unless otherwise credited.

First published 2014

Amberley Publishing
The Hill, Stroud
Gloucestershire, GL5 4EP

www.amberley-books.com

Copyright © Geoff Swaine, 2014

The right of Geoff Swaine to be identified as
the Author of this work has been asserted in
accordance with the Copyrights, Designs and
Patents Act 1988.

ISBN 978 1 4456 3945 1 (print)
ISBN 978 1 4456 3956 7 (ebook)

British Library Cataloguing in Publication Data.
A catalogue record for this book is available from
the British Library.

Typesetting by Amberley Publishing.
Printed in the UK.

Contents

Introduction

We now have a preservation movement in Britain which is the envy of the world. It shows how the love and admiration of the steam engine was taken forward and not allowed to die.

The volunteer force of preservationists has made their mark on the industrial history of this country and their personal sacrifices will be remembered by the generations to come. With over 100 heritage railways active at the moment, the sites have proved a magnet for visitors, young and old.

It is now a good time to look at what we have because after some forty years of operation, those early pioneers are handing over, or have handed over, to the next generation, and the new people are ready, willing and able to carry on the good work.

Part of the reason why the heritage lines are doing so well is because the steam engine was so quickly and thoroughly disposed of in the early 1960s. Steam locomotive lovers stood dumbfounded in the wake of seeing these 'wonders of motion' so radically discarded. Some, like the British Standard 9Fs, had only been in operation for a year or two when the mass slaughter of the steam engines went ahead. Alright, we know that the steam engine had to be replaced sometime, but all that we were being left were static exhibits in a museum.

Those fine people who found they were in the right place to make inroads into saving an engine or a section of track led the way. For, within a few years others were taking up the mantle to do the same. Many local authorities encouraged the idea, for preserved lines were a new venture and added a new tourist attraction to the area. It soon became apparent that not only did the new railways become popular with tourists but, in some locations, they revived a whole town. The war-revival events soon spread from the confines of the preserved railways to become a major attraction in a calendar of events. Everyone in these areas now gets into the act of recreating a little bit of the past, even if it is just for one day a year.

By the early 1970s, dozens of lines were being revived and refitted with reclaimed artefacts which had become redundant from the steam era, but had not by that time been disposed of. Quite often a derelict station building from somewhere would be purchased; then would come the job of dismantling it and rebuilding it in its new location at a heritage line. The same thing happened with signal boxes, sheds, watering equipment and anything else which could be found to perform a function.

So many lines had sprung up that it soon became obvious that there was an acute shortage of one particular item, something that had been scrapped in the thousands. That was, of course, the steam engine. Anything saveable from factory workings or docks had been claimed, as had some of the former GWR pannier tank engines; these had been bought by London Transport from BR Western Region a few years earlier to perform shunting duties around their sidings in north-west London. One of these, No. LT94 (WR7752), had performed the last task in steam days. That was by taking a train through the tunnels below London's Euston Road in June 1971.

The shortage of engines did, though, have a solution. There was the store of derelict steam locomotives which had accumulated in a scrap yard on Barry Island, South Wales. This was under the ownership of Dai Woodham, who by chance had cut up trucks and wagons before turning his attention to the steam engines. Enthusiasts got hold of this information and went there to see what was going on. Unfortunately, these locos had been sitting out in the open for a good few years, exposed to the sea air.

For a while the enthusiasts only claimed a few items from these hulks, which, by this time, had generally been reduced to lace. So desperate was this new industry for steam engines that one or two of the better examples got taken up. They got taken away to their new homes, for small groups of dedicated people to start work on. If two of the same type were taken, one could be a donor for the other, thereby solving a problem of missing parts. However, it was mostly found that new parts would have to be manufactured to replace what was missing or rotten. Sometimes it was just the wheels, frame and cab which were left standing and reusable from the reclaimed engine.

Word must have got round that it was possible to restore these old, scrapped locos, because a steady stream started to be bought from this stock. Dai Woodham obviously thought this was good business, for it was much easier to sell an item rather to go to the trouble of breaking it up.

Incredibly, out of 297 engines which came through this yard, 213 were saved. A whole new band of preservationists came on board to learn and provide the skills necessary for this task.

With the location of the scrap yard being where it is, the selection of locomotives which had been sent there reflected that side of the country – only one example from British Railways Eastern Region came from it. That was former LNER B1 (now running as BR No. 61264). But, never mind – this stock of engines went on to make up the shortfall of this prime piece of equipment, with the last one being removed in January 1990. This was GWR Prairie Tank No. 5553.

We all now have the pleasure in visiting these railways, with the thought that our money given at the gate continues to keep it all alive.

GNR N2 No. 1744 powers under the road bridge with the train out of Weybourne on the North Norfolk Railway, destination Cuffley.

City of Truro, coupled with *Earl of Berkeley*, double-heads a service out of Ropley heading towards Medstead and Four Marks.

19 Ex-SECR 'C' Class No. 592 (BR 31592). The evening sunlight catches the sumptuous Edwardian livery during a Branch Line Weekend as she runs back into service.

BS 9F 2-10-0 No. 92203 *Black Prince* brings a northbound train into Toddington station at the Gloucestershire Warwickshire Railway. Note the wildlife foundation sign on the front.

West Somerset Railway

Above left: Somerset & Dorset Joint Railway Fowler No. 88 in distinctive Prussian blue livery.

Above right: Royal Scot at the end of the line, Minehead.

Left: No. 4936 *Kinlet Hall* on the turntable at Minehead.

Black 5 No. 45231 *The Sherwood Forester* lets off considerable steam in the early morning sun at Minehead station. Meanwhile, at the other end of the day, newly restored 4-6-2 No. 6100 *Royal Scot* runs out of service at Minehead station. This engine was formerly No. 6152 *The King's Dragoon Guardsman*, whose identity was changed before her trip to the USA and Canada in 1933, but never changed back.

Above: Definitely not a vacuum-operated device, the newly installed turntable at Minehead gets turned by some good old-fashioned muscle power. The engine on the turntable is GWR Hall Class No. 4936 *Kinlet Hall.*

Below: No. 4936 stands by in the preparation area at Minehead station.

Above: Making a magnificent sight, Black 5 No. 45231 *The Sherwood Forester* and Light Pacific No. 34036 *Braunton* take the train from Williton up the rise towards the A358 road bridge.

Below: At the same location, GWR Mogul No. 9351 leads Fowler No. 88 on a spirited run past Castle Hill and over the road bridge.

Bluebell Railway

Above left: Ex-SECR C Class No. 592 waits with a train at Horsted Keynes.

Above right: South Eastern Railway Stirling 0-6-0 No. 65. Built in 1896, the engine now has a new ticket to run again in service.

DS 377, also known as BR 3 Stroudley Terrier 2655 *Stepney*, repainted into Stroudley's famous 'Improved Engine Green' (which is not green).

Above: Rebuilt Battle of Britain Class No. 34059 *Sir Archibald Sinclair* runs into the station at Sheffield Park.

Right: No. 34059 finds a shaft of sunlight as she moves northward through the tree-lined cutting outside Horsted Keynes station.

Above: 'Dukedog' No. 9017 at the preparation area at Sheffield Park station. The 1938 rebuild of 9017 used the frames from Bulldog No. 3425 (built 1906) and the boiler and cab from Duke Class No. 3282 (built in 1899).

Below: No. 9017 runs through at Horsted Keynes with the Pullman dining train. The engine is turned out minus the *Earl of Berkeley* nameplates, a name she was given while already in preservation. The name *Earl Berkeley* was actually allocated to Castle Class No. 5060, since scrapped.

Above: Fairburn Tank 2-6-4T No. 42085 on its first visit to the Bluebell Railway from the Lakeside & Haverthwaite Railway. Built at Brighton for use on the Southern Region in 1951, this style of large tank engine was first developed in the late 1920s, to be perpetuated by many CMEs afterwards.

Below: The British Standard version No. 80151 – an engine which was rescued from the Barry scrapyard in 1974.

North York Moors Railway

Above left: LMS Black 5 No. 45212 in the evening sunlight at Grosmont.

Above right: British Standard Class 4, 2-6-0 No. 76079, known as the 'Pocket Rocket'.

Original cast-iron rails for horse-drawn trains.

Above: Ex-LNER A4 Pacific 60007 *Sir Nigel Gresley* runs around at Pickering to the admiration of all spectators, no matter what age. In the background is the ensign of English Heritage flying above Pickering Castle.

Below: A1 Peppercorn Pacific No. 60163 *Tornado* has arrived with her train. Awestruck youngsters and 'knowledgeable' older people are enjoying the sheer theatre that surrounds the performance of a big steam engine.

Two examples of post-nationalisation liveries. The A4, 60007 *Sir Nigel Gresley*, is in the short-lived (1949/51) BR livery of blue given to engines of designation 8P. Meanwhile, below, in the same location at Pickering station, the all-new Peppercorn A1 No. 60163 *Tornado* waits, sporting a livery of apple green. The authorities allowed some of the former 'Big 4' liveries to continue for a while before the standard colours came in.

A1 Peppercorn Pacific (4-6-2 wheel arrangement) No. 60163 *Tornado* arrives at Pickering. Her badge commemorates the flying corps from the first Gulf War. Previously a badge was only added to this class if the name represented a pre-grouping railway company, i.e. 'Great Northern'. This engine was built from new by a group of enthusiasts at Darlington to make up an example of a class where none were preserved.

Didcot Railway Centre

Above left: A classic branch-line scene sees diesel railcar No. 22 pass the signal box on the branch line.

Above right: The completely new power unit for 'Railmotor' No. 93.

Below left: The front end of 'Railmotor' with power unit installed.

Below right: Broad gauge and standard gauge come together at these points, which makes for rather an interesting study.

The dark smoke indicates that fresh coal has just been applied to the fire. No. 5322 Mogul (2-6-0) makes a fine sight on the Didcot express line. 43xx Class 2-6-0 No. 5322 was built in 1917. With the ROD (Railway Operating Division) markings, she would have been shipped to France for war use from new. In the First World War even the engines had to wear khaki!

Replica *Fire Fly* fits into the bigger arch of the transfer shed while the other arch is sized for 'narrow' stock, as the Western railwaymen liked to call them. The shed dates from 1863 and was rescued from another part of Didcot. The original track comes from Burlescombe, Devon, where it was found buried.

Completed at Didcot in 2005, the 2-2-2 new-build loco has since been the only regular operational example of Brunel's broad gauge system.

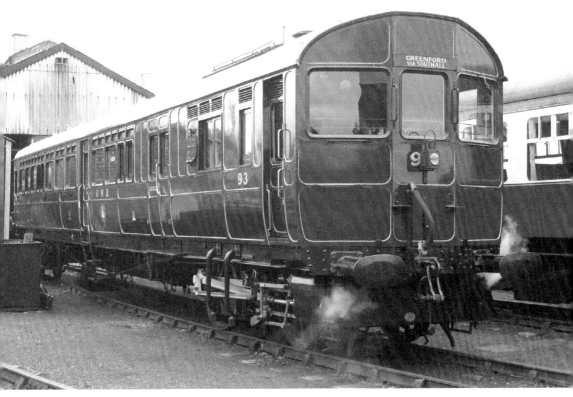

Above: Two classic railcars at Didcot. The 1908-built 'Railmotor' No. 93 stands at the Didcot centre. Originally outshopped from Swindon Works in 1908, the self-propelled vehicle looks in great shape.

Below: Diesel railcar No. 22 waits in a sunny spot before being taken into service. The GWR diesel railcars are loved by enthusiasts, while the DMUs, which replaced steam on suburban services, are mostly despised.

Fire Fly and her replica train are now regular performers at the Didcot Railway Centre. An operator worked the disc and crossbar signal from below in early broad gauge days. After a train had passed he would wait six minutes before giving another train clearance. After 1852 they were operated by overhead wires.

Dual-gauge line work runs from the transfer shed, where goods would be transferred from a train of one gauge to the other.

A classic branch-line scene from the Great Western Railway sees diesel railcar No. 22 move into Didcot terminus station. There is also an earlier version of the GWR diesel railcar, which was introduced in 1934. This had rounded, rather than angular, front features and just one engine.

The renowned Ransomes & Rapier Ltd of Ipswich have left their mark with the turntable at Didcot.

Mid-Hants Railway (Watercress Line)

Above left: The classic lines of A4 *Bittern* are seen on the embankment heading towards Ropley.

Above right: *City of Truro* is seen here coupled with *Earl of Berkeley* double-heading a service towards Medstead & Four Marks.

Below left: Metropolitan Railway 0-4-4 'E' No. 1 beside the watering point at Ropley.

Below right: LN Class *Lord Nelson* with head plate 'The Cunarder', named after the notable boat train which ran from London's Waterloo station to the Southampton Ocean Terminal.

Action at the Bowers Green Bridge between Ropley and Medstead & Four Marks on the 'Watercress Line'. *Lord Nelson* approaches with a service towards Ropley before making way for the following service with BS Class 2MT No. 41312 tank in charge. This is the 2-6-2T tank version of the Ivatt 'Mickey Mouse' tender engine. This post-war design allowed all the much older pre-Grouping tanks to be scrapped.

Above: If it weren't for the photographers, this picture could have been taken in 1949. Two engines are shown, both with their roots in Victorian times. This time it is GWR Dukedog *Earl of Berkeley* taking the lead position for a double-headed service out of Ropley.

Below: Great Western Hall Class *Pitchford Hall* and BS Class 5 depart to a cacophony of sound.

Above: No. 850 *Lord Nelson*. The four-cylindered motion of *Lord Nelson* has a sound and beat all of its own. When first introduced in 1926, this prototype was hailed as the most powerful 4-6-0 locomotive in Britain. The livery is the Bulleid favourite – malachite green.

Below: Designed to haul the heaviest boat trains from London to all the South Coast ports, No. 850 (BR 30850) is seen here heading a breakdown train into Ropley station.

British Standard Types

British Standard Variations Produced from 1951

A total of 999 examples were produced, and all were designed by Robert Riddles, who was, in all but name, the Chief Mechanical Engineer for British Railways. Riddles was an ex-London Midland Scottish Railway man who worked under William Stanier, so it came as no surprise that his engines were a development of that railway's designs. The Power Classification was also incorporated from that railway, and classified locomotives according to their power on a grade from one to ten, ten being the most powerful. The lowest British Standard Type had a classification of two, and then the rest followed as such. There were twelve BS types in all:

1. 84xxx Class 2, 2-6-2T, based on Ivatt Class 2 tank. Thirty built.
None preserved. New example being created at Bluebell Railway using 78059 as a donor.
2. 82xxx Class 3, 2-6-2T, tank version of the 77xxx type. Forty-five built.
None preserved. New-build in progress at Severn Valley Railway.
3. 78xx Class 2, 2-6-0, Standard Ivatt Class 2 type. Sixty-five built.
Five in preservation.
4. 80xxx Class 3, 2-6-4T, the well-liked Fowler/Stanier/Fairburn design continued. 155 built.
Fifteen in preservation.
5. 77xxx Class 3, 2-6-0, for lightly laid routes. Twenty built.
All extinct.
6. 76xxx Class 4, 2-6-0, based on the heavier Ivatt Class 4. Tender incorporates back of cab. 115 built.
Four in preservation.
7. 75xxx Class 4, 4-6-0. Introduced to replace the 'Manor' Class of the GWR with the Cambrian coast route in mind. Eighty built.
Six survive in preservation.
Also a 4-6-0 76xxx version – 115 built with 4 preserved.
8. 73xxx Class 5, 4-6-0, designed to complement the Black 5 Class of the LMS. 172 built. Nos 73125–73154 had Caprotti valve-gear fitted.
Five in preservation: Nos 73050, 73082, 73096, 73129 and 73156.
9. 72xxx 'Clan', 4-6-2, a lighter version of the Britannia. Ten built (used mostly in Scotland).
None survived. One new-build under construction.
10. The 70xxx Britannia, 4-6-2 (two-cylinder) Class. Fifty built.
Two Preserved: 70000 *Britannia* and 70013 *Oliver Cromwell*.
11. The 71xxx, 4-6-2 (three-cylinder) Class. Just one example: No. 71000, *Duke of Gloucester*.
Preserved.
12. 9F 92xxx 2-10-0 built for heavy freight but also used for passenger services. 251 built.
Nine survive in preservation.

Two British Standard classes at the Midland Railway Centre. Above: BR Standard Class 5MT 4-6-0 No. 73129 was built at Derby loco works in 1956. It was a class designed to supersede the Black 5s.

Below: 9F No. 92214, a design by Robert Riddles to replicate his highly successful WD 2-10-0 Class.

Llangollen Railway

The driver of the Auto-train brings it into the station.

Interesting geometric shape – the footbridge at Llangollen station.

Four-wheeled diesel Railbus heads upgrade towards Berwyn tunnel.

Above: All the skills of the driver are required not only to stop the train in the station at Berwyn, but also to get it going again. Black 5 No. 44806 heads up grade out of Berwyn station with the afternoon service.

Below: With the bright evening sunlight shining on the north face of Berwyn station, Black 5 No. 44806 powers up the steep Berwyn bank. This is the 18.30 Real Ale Special out of Llangollen.

Black 5 No. 44806 lies in wait at Llangollen station. This engine has the name *Kenneth Aldcroft*, an honorary title applied in the days of preservation. The class, designed by Stanier of the LMS in the thirties, is probably the most successful and most respected 'general duty' engine ever made. Visually they have a pleasing compactness about them.

Above: With the driver visible in the cab vestibule, the Auto-train makes a splendid sight, having just left Glyndyfrdwy and heading up grade towards Berwyn tunnel. The line hugs the River Dee through the valley.

Below: The Auto-train with the engine in the middle of a four-carriage set. The driver controls the regulator in the engine by means of connecting rods under the carriage.

Keighley & Worth Valley Railway

LMS Fowler 'Jinty' tank 47279 pilots Taff Vale Railway tank No. 65 away from Keighley station with a passenger service.

Above: WD 2-8-0 90733 is at the back of the train moving empty stock at the start of the day. Here, the train is approaching Oakworth.

Below: Midland Railway Fowler 0-6-0, built in 1920. The class became a mainstay of the LMS after 'grouping', and was called upon for all duties except pulling the heaviest trains. Here, one example, No. 43924, is catching the early evening sunshine head on while approaching Ingrow station.

Above: BR Britannia Class No. 70013 *Oliver Cromwell* attacks the 1 in 58 gradient out of Keighley station. Fifty-five of this class were built. This example got saved because she was active right up to the end of steam in 1968.

Below: LMS Fowler 'Jinty' tank 47279 (built 1924) heads away from the station.

Above: WD 90733 is led out of Keighley station by Ivatt tank No. 41241 with the 15.55 buffet service.

Below: Oakworth Village Morris Dancers perform on Keighley station before boarding the train.

Great Central Railway

Above left: No. 30777 *Sir Lamiel* picks up speed out of the station as she heads for the double-track section of line.

Above right: Robinson No. 63601, 2-8-0, prepares to head a service out of Loughborough station.

Left: No. 30777 *Sir Lamiel* is seen outside the Loughborough works.

Above: A visitor to the GCR is Southern Railway Schools Class *Cheltenham*. Originally introduced in 1930, these engines were designed to cope with the severe width restrictions of the London–Hastings line.

Below: The three-cylinder Schools Class No. 925 in 'Bulleid Period' malachite green. Wheel arrangement 4-4-0 fronts up to the Beavertail coach E1719E (built in Doncaster in 1937).

48624 8F 2-8-0, built at Ashford in 1943 for the war effort, just as the Robinson 2-8-0 was previously selected as the standard war engine. The Stanier design was adopted by the War Department as the foremost engine for heavy haulage during the Second World War, and they were used at home and abroad. In splendid maroon livery the 8F heads her train of all-steel mineral goods wagons along the racing stretch of double trackwork towards Quorn & Woodhouse.

Introduced by Ivatt in 1946, 46521 was one of the last being outshopped from Swindon in 1953. Of the Mogul wheel arrangement – 2-6-0 – they were very suited to either passenger or freight work. Here the 2MT engine runs tender first towards Quorn with a fitted freight. So good were they that Robin Riddles copied them for his British Standard Types in the fifties. Below is one such example, No. 78019 2-6-0 Standard Class 2, 1954.

The 9400 Class was the last of the Panniers to be introduced by Hawksworth and built by the GWR (WR) between 1947 and 1956. Here at Loughborough, the powerful tapered-boiler engine waits to take forward the postal special. The picture below shows all the paraphernalia that can be on a station. Under the bridge is an original air-raid shelter.

Above: Robinson 2-8-0, No. 63601, waits to take out a service from Loughborough. This engine is the only surviving example in this country.

Below: The train is seen powering away from Loughborough station with a southbound service.

Severn Valley Railway

The Duke shines out in late afternoon sun crossing the Victoria Bridge. BR Standard Class No. 71000 *Duke of Gloucester* was built in 1954 as a class of one locomotive.

Above: '4500 Class' 2-6-2T No. 4566 *Small Prairie* was built at Swindon in 1929 and designed by Churchward. One of a class of seventy-five to have a flat-top water tank. Class 4575, with the slightly larger water tanks, were introduced in 1927.

Below: No. 7812 *Erlestoke Manor* stands in front of sister engine No. 7802 *Bradley Manor* at the end of the day.

Above: No. 71000 *Duke of Gloucester* passes the distinctive rake of Severn Valley's Gresley teak-bodied coaches at Bewdley station.

Below: Ivatt Mogul No. 46443 at Bridgnorth shed after a day of service. Built in 1950 at Crewe, she was one of a class introduced in 1946. The railwaymen of the forties used to nickname this class 'Mickey Mouse', because of the fragility of their appearance.

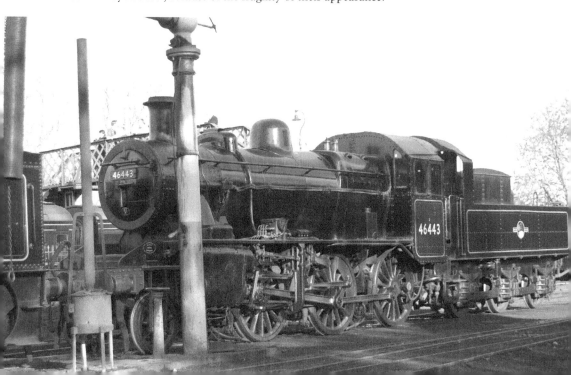

Above: Those fabulous wheels of the Duke are so close at the Bridgnorth depot. Note the universal joints on the Caprotti valve-gear connecting rod.

Below: No. 71000 *Duke of Gloucester* serenely brings her train along the embankment towards Bridgnorth.

North Norfolk Railway

Above left: An American serviceman and companion travelling inside the Quad-Art set.

Above right: Happy 'period' travellers share a compartment.

Below left: An SS officer and wife on Sheringham station!

Below right: Home Guard soldiers run through some drills in front of WD 2-10-0, 90775.

The Riddles-designed WD 2-10-0, 90775, built in 1943 to complement the WD 2-8-0s; the Ministry of Supply wanted heavy goods engines. With the larger wheelbase, the 2-10-0s had a lighter axel loading than the eight-coupled type. Robert Riddles designed the WDs to last just a couple of years, but both types lasted close to the end of steam. Riddles perpetuated the style when selecting British Standard types, as below with 9F 92203 at Sheringham station.

Two engines with a London connection. N7 0-6-2T, originally No. 999, the last engine built at Stratford in 1921, being ordered by the GER. The engine was numbered 69621 by BR after nationalisation, and the class was scheduled for the intensive Liverpool Street suburban services. Both engines cross at Weybourne for this special situation. The plate on the side of the N2 tells us that the engine was built at the Hyde Park works, Glasgow, in 1921.

B12 2-6-0 BR No. 61572, 1928. The original Holden design was in 1911 for the GER, and had a wheel arrangement of 4-4-0. Rebuilt by Gresley to Class B12/3, No. 8572 was completed in 1928. Now it has a larger boiler and six-coupled driving wheels in the space where there were originally four. Here we see the B12 in action on the rise out of Sheringham and at the end of the line at Holt station.

In subterranean form departing from Weybourne with the 14.15 service, the GNR N2 No. 1744 powers under the road bridge. These engines were designed for work within the tunnels of the Metropolitan Railway near King's Cross station. Generally, however, they powered just about all the short-haul suburban services in and around King's Cross until 1962.

Above: The visiting N2 engine is seen here in the green livery in which she entered service for the Great Northern Railway in 1921. An attentive audience watches every move as the train departs Weybourne for Holt. The guard watches the smoke and steam clear as the N2 gathers speed for the final leg of the journey.

Below: The destination on the side of the train does not match that on the front, but never mind. The acrobat signal indicates a clear road ahead.

Kent & East Sussex Railway

One end of a Wainwright 'Birdcage' carriage from 1910 with its distinctive lookout.

A Vintage train is approaching the Cranbrook Road crossing.

Above: British Standard 4 Tank Engine No. 80072 is the guest engine on this day. On loan from the Llangollen Railway, the engine formally worked on the suburban services out of Fenchurch Street station, London.

Below: The nine-engine cavalcade glows in the spring sunshine for the early start of the spring gala.

Above: The locomotive built in 1917 by Manning Wardle brings up the rear of the cavalcade.

Below: The side view of SR USA Class No. 65 clearly shows the engine's very short wheelbase, which is one of the reasons why it was well suited for working the sharp curves around the former Southampton Dock lines.

Morris dancers perform at Tenterden station, while, below, the enginemen and enginewomen of the nine-engine parade at Tenterden have taken their places for a proud picture, and now disperse to get the day underway. Note the enginemen wearing ties – the proud old traditions still exist.

Engines for War

In the same way as the Robinson GCR 2-8-0 engine was selected as the most suitable locomotive for the heavy freight trains required for war transportation back in the First World War, the LMS 8F 2-8-0 was selected by the Ministry of Supply as the standard machine for the Second World War. Further designs on the same theme were required, and the task of development was given to R. A. Riddles. He promptly introduced an 'austerity' 2-8-0 engine to supplement the 8F.

A total of 935 of the WD 2-8-0s were produced from 1943, with the thought that they would only have a lifespan of two years; how wrong could they have been? Overall 733 of these machines passed into the hands of British Railways on nationalisation in 1948, with most lasting until the end of steam. So humdrum were they thought to be that none achieved preservation status. The Worth Valley Railway tracked down one example that had escaped the cutter's torch – in Sweden. They managed to get it back to Keighley, where it can now be seen regularly heading trains along the line.

Although the 2-8-0 8Fs and WD versions were successful engines, their axle loading put limitations on their use, which demanded that another locomotive should be introduced. The Ministry of Supply wanted a powerful heavy freight engine for use at home and abroad. It needed to be able to work over lightly laid track, or lines with weak bridges, and should therefore have an axle loading of not more than 13 tons.

Riddles' answer was a 2-10-0 locomotive, of which 150 were built, all at the Hyde Park works, Glasgow. Most did service in Britain before being taken abroad to help with the Allied liberation of Europe.

The only drawback with a set of ten coupled driving wheels was the radius of a curve that the engine could take. To help overcome this restriction, the centre wheels were made flangeless, and the second and fourth driving wheels were shallow-flanged. Other innovations were incorporated, such as a wide firebox and rocking grate, for easy removal of the fire remains.

The North Yorkshire Moors Railway runs two examples of this class, both of which came back to Britain from Greece in 1984. No. 90775 was formerly WD601, named *Sturdee*, while WD 3672 *Dame Vera Lynn* saw war service in Egypt.

Some spartan fittings were used in the manufacture of these engines, such as a tiny chimney and cast front wheels. These really did give them their 'austere' appearance. They were designed for speed of manufacture, and prefabricated parts were used wherever possible.

One other notable example in preservation is No. 600 *Gordon*. This is now in storage with the Severn Valley Railway, and was originally a training locomotive on the Longmoor Military Railway.

R. A. Riddles was to become Chief Mechanical Engineer (or the equivalent) of the newly formed British Railways in 1948. He was instrumental in producing the British Standard types, and one of those was the 9F 2-10-0 Class. It was obvious from the many similarities that the 9F design was based on his wartime version.

Above: Heavy-duty goods engines designed for war. *Above:* 2-8-0 WD 90733 from the Keighley & Worth Valley Railway.

Below: The slightly later variant, which has a lighter axle loading and better route availability. WD 3672 *Dame Vera Lynne* is currently out of service at the North York Moors Railway.

Gloucestershire Warwickshire Railway

Above left: British Standard 9F No. 92203 *Black Prince* 2-10-0 (1959) celebrated its fiftieth birthday with a fly-past by a Spitfire. No. 92203 was purchased by David Shepherd straight out of British Railways service.

Above right: David Shepherd stands proudly beside his charge.

No. 92203 *Black Prince* exits Greet tunnel and approaches Winchcombe station.

BR Standard Class 9, 2-10-0, was designed for heavy freight trains but was to show a good turn of speed when put to use on passenger services. The flangeless centre wheels gave it good route accessibility. Here, *Black Prince* is at Winchcombe station being prepared for the last leg of her journey.

GWR No. 3440 *City of Truro* 4-4-0, 1903, moves to the coaling area at Torrington on the Gloucestershire Warwickshire Railway. The innovation of Churchward's tapered boiler on his predecessor's double-framed 4-4-0 design clearly shows the evolution of this remarkable loco.

The Dean-pattern outside frame, coupling-rod crank and outside-framed bogie firmly place this design in the Victorian age. The technologies of the broad gauge era are still apparent in this design. *City of Truro* shows the elaborate insignia from Edwardian times on her tender. This was the 'golden' age of steam travel.

Bo'ness and Kinneil Railway

Sir Nigel Gresley stops off at the Bo'ness Railway during a tour of the country in 2011. The train here is marshalled as a push-pull unit for the journey between Bo'ness and Manuel. Now the Gresley A4 is on the home stretch into Bo'ness station.

Above: A sure-fire way of keeping the children happy is to front a train with a little blue engine. The enthusiast will also be happy because LNER's *Sir Nigel Gresley* is on the back.

Below: LNER No. 13803 (1946) teak-simulated open third coach is being shunted through the overall-roofed station at Bo'ness. This is a design of Gresley tradition.

Above: Sir Nigel Gresley has some attention before regaining 'her' place at the end of the train.

Below: J36 0-6-0 Class engine *Maude* makes an appearance at Bo'ness station. This is the locomotive that appeared in the later making of *The Railway Children*.

Above: The mist rolls in across the Firth of Forth, but the Gresley A4 makes a spectacular sight bathed in sunlight. The train approaches the site of the former Bo'ness station.

Below: Sir Nigel Gresley puts on a spectacular show at Bo'ness station.

Battlefield Line

Definitely the end of the line. Class B1 *Mayflower* is about to run around the train to complete the last service of the day. In the background are the shed and support stock area for the railway. That point is also where the line divides.

These items are now industrial antiques.

This fine collection of 'railwayana' is in the Shackerstone museum, housed in the fine Victorian station building. The collection, which is now surely complete, was put together by the railway's former signalman, John C. Jacques MBE.

Above: Thompson LNER Class B1 No. 1306 (BR 61306) *Mayflower* (1948), brings home a service into Shackerstone station. The engine is representative of pre-nationalisation livery – LNER lined apple green.

Below: The original ornate Victorian station building is still here and fully restored.

Above: Mayflower prepares to uncouple from her train.

Below: Thompson LNER Class B1 No. 1306 (BR 61306) *Mayflower* (1948) runs around after bringing home a service into Shackerstone station.

Spa Valley Railway

A close comparison can be made here at the Spa Valley Railway between a pannier tank and one of the popular 'Jinties'. No. 47493 was built at the Vulcan Foundry Ltd in 1928. Reversing through the woods below is a long wheelbase LT works train, headed by London Transport pannier tank L99. This view is closed off once the leaves arrive.

Above: Looking on with great interest at the miniature tube train is Polish-built Type Tkh Works No. 3135 *Spartan*, imported into this country in 1997.

Below: A 'Jinty'. No. 47493 was built at the Vulcan Foundry Ltd in 1928. This class was so reliable that they became the mainstay of the post 'Grouping' company London Midland Scottish Railway. They were to the LMS what the panniers were to the GWR.

57xx 0-6-0PT (former GWR No. 7715) was part of an allocation sold to London Transport between 1956 and 1963. With that department she carried the number L99. Her sister engine, L94 (7752), was the last steam engine to take a train through the tunnels of the Metropolitan Railway on 16 June 1971, thereby effectively ending steam services in Britain. L94 runs here on the Spa Valley Railway, and is resplendent after a repaint in LT colours.

East Lancs Railway

Hughes/Fowler 'Crab' 2-6-0 stands in the impressive Rawtenstall station.

Above: Examples of old luggage on show at the East Lancs Railway; these are always popular items to adorn a platform.

Below: BR blue-liveried diesel No. 55022 *Royal Scots Grey* with arrow logo, which came in from 1966, about to pass around to the front for the next service out of Rawtenstall. The architecture on the railway is true to its traditions. The clock tower here at Rawtenstall was designed to resemble the tower of the former Bury station.

Above: Resident at this railway, BS Class No. 71000 *Duke of Gloucester* (here seen at Rawtenstall) has been a triumph for the preservation movement, as it had steaming problems when first produced. It was the enthusiasts who took the engine from the scrapyard at Barry Island and rebuilt her, solving all the problems along the way.

Below: British Standard Class 4 No. 80080 has arrived at Ramsbottom station.

Above: BS Class 4 tank 2-6-4T No. 80080 continues to wait, but the train from the north does arrive.

Below: BS Class No. 71000 *Duke of Gloucester* has arrived at Ramsbottom with the southbound service, which enables the train with the BS tank to get under way. The BS tank is showing the shed plate No. 33A – Plaistow on the smokebox door. This reminds us that she worked the London, Tilbury & Southend line, where she linked up with three-cylinder Stanier and Fairburn engines of similar design to provide a great swansong of steam right up to 1962, when steam gave way to electrification on the line.

Nene Valley Railway

Replica of Locomotion No. 1 on show at the Nene Valley Railway.

This and next page: The railway always strives to attract the enthusiast visitor, as is evident here with a double LNER attraction. *Mayflower* and *Green Arrow* are both in action at Wansford.

German-built ex-Polish State Railways 2-10-0 No. 7173, the largest engine that has run in preservation. Now, sadly, it is unlikely to be seen running again, due to its size and running costs.

British Standard 5, 4-6-0 (built 1954), is the design intended to replace the Black 5s. No. 73050 backs on to her train, named *City of Peterborough*; the engine has become the flagship of the railway. The last passengers board the train before the British Standard loco takes the train forward towards Peterborough.

Above: Polish 5485, 0-8-0T, engine heads a train across the River Nene towards Wansford station, viewed from the picnic area.

Below: The Polish engine 5485 heads a service out of Wansford station. Note the predominant Continental stock. Many film companies have used these when a 'Continental' scene is required.

Isle of Wight Steam Railway

This and next page: The perfect sight on a southern steam heritage railway is a Stroudley Terrier. Looking splendid in authentic green livery, ex-LBSCR No. 8 *Freshwater* switches platforms at Havenstreet.

Opposite top: The Adams-designed 0-4-4T '02' No. W24 *Calbourne* is back in operation after a wait of eight years. This class was a favourite for performing shunting duties at Waterloo station in the 1950s and 1960s. Here an example is seen returned to its 1950 livery, complete with large bunker and early BR crest. *Opposite bottom:* The nine-compartment third-class carriage No. S2416 stands after disgorging its passengers. Not one carriage less than seventy-five years old operates on the IoW Steam Railway.

Bodmin & Wenford Railway

A fine pairing of two West Country stalwarts. *Greyhound* LSWR T9 No. 30120 (SR number), piloted by Well Tank 30587, makes the approach to Bodmin Town. The engines have the early BR livery of 'blackberry' black.

Above: Greyhound No. 30120 waiting at the watering facility at Bodmin General station. Note the high water capacity 'bunker' tender to the engine.

Below: Well Tank No. 30587 waiting at the water facility at Bodmin General station. Originally designed for London work by Beattie, three examples found their way to Cornwall to work the Wadebridge–Wenford Bridge mineral line; two have survived.

South Devon Railway

Above: The attractive station building at Buckfastleigh.

Below: Collett 2251 Class, designed for mixed traffic. In unlined BR green livery, the engine heads into Buckfastleigh station. No. 3205 is the only survivor of a class of 120.

Dartmouth Steam Railway & Riverboat Company

Above: The signage at Paignton station shows the new combined offering of the railway. The station is alongside the main-line station.

Below: Two sister engines run on this railway. Here, No. 4277, 4200 Class, *Hercules* coasts a homebound service down the grade beside Goodrington Sands.

Schedule of Lines (Standard Gauge)

Alderney Railway
Alderney, C.I.
www.alderneyrailway.com
Tel: 01455 634373

Avon Valley Railway
Bitton Station, Near Bristol,
BS30 6HD
www.avonvalleyrailway.org.uk
Tel: 01457 484950

Barrow Hill Roundhouse
Chesterfield, Derbyshire, S43
2PR
www.barrowhill.org.uk
Tel: 01246 472450

Barry Tourist Railway
www.barrytouristrailway.co.uk
Tel: 01446748816

Battlefield Line Railway
Shackerstone Station, CV13
6NW
www.battlefield-line-railway.
co.uk
Tel: 01827 880754

Birmingham Railway Museum
670 Warwick Road, Tyseley,
B11 2HL
www.tyseleylocoworks.co.uk
Vintage Trains Tel: 01217
084960

Bluebell Railway
Sheffield Park Station, TN22
3QL
Horsted Keynes Station, RH17
7BB
www.bluebell-railway.co.uk
Tel: 01825 720800

Bodmin and Wenford Railway
Bodmin General Station, PL31
1AQ
www.bodminrailway.co.uk
Tel: 01208 73666

Bo'ness and Kinneil Railway
Bo'ness Station, EH51 9AQ
www.bkrailway.co.uk
Tel: 01506 825855

Bowes Railway Centre
Gateshead, NE9 7QJ
www.newcastlegateshead.com
Tel: 01914 161847

Bressingham Steam Museum
Near Diss, Norfolk, IP22 2AA
www.bressingham.co.uk
Tel: 01379 686900

Bristol Harbour Railway
Princes Wharf, BS1 4RN
www.bristolharbourrailway.
co.uk
Tel: 01173 526600

Buckingham Railway Centre
Quainton Road Station, HP22
4BY
www.bucksrailcentre.org.uk
Tel: 01296 655720

Caledonian Railway
Brechin Station, DD97AF
www.caledonian-railway.com
Tel: 01356 622992

Chasewater Railway
Brownhills West, WS8 7NL
www.chasewaterrailway.co.uk
Tel: 01543 452623

Chinnor & Princes Risborough
Railway
Chinnor Station, OX39 4ER
www.chinnorrailway.co.uk
Talking Timetable: 01844
353535

Cholsey & Wallingford
Railway
Wallingford, OX10 9GQ
www.cholsey-wallingford-

railway.com
Tel: 01491 835067

Churnet Valley Railway
Kingsley & Froghall Station,
ST10 2HA
www.churnet-valley-railway.
org.uk
Tel: 01538 750755

Colne Valley Railway
Castle Hedingham, CO9 3DZ
www.colnevalleyrailway.co.uk
Tel: 01787 461174

Darlington Railway Museum
Station Rd, Darlington, DL3
6ST
www.darlington.gov.uk
Tel: 01325 460532

Dartmoor Railway
Oakhampton, EX20 1EJ
www.dartmoorrailway.com
Tel: 01837 55164

Dartmouth Steam Railway &
River Boat Company
Paignton, TQ4 6AF
www.dartmouthrailriver.co.uk
Tel: 01803 555872

Dean Forest Railway
Lydney, GL15 4ET
www.deanforestrailway.co.uk
Tel: 01594 845840

Derwentvalley Light Railway
Murton Park, York, YO19 5UF
www.dvlr.org.uk
Tel: 01904 489966

Didcot Railway Centre
Didcot, OX11 7NJ
www.didcotrailwaycentre.
org.uk
Tel: 01235 817200

Downpatrick & Co. Down
Railway
Downpatrick Station, N.I.,
BT30 6LZ
www.downrail.co.uk
Tel: 02844 612233

East Anglian Railway Museum
Chappel, Near Colchester,
CO6 2DS
www.earm.co.uk
Tel: 01206 242524

East Kent Railway
Shepherdswell, CT15 7PD
www.eastkentrailway.co.uk
Tel: 01304 832042

East Somerset Railway
Cranmore Station, BA4 4QP
www.eastsomersetrailway.
co.uk
Tel: 01749 880417

East Lancashire Railway
Bury Bolton Street Station, BL9
0EY

Rawtenstall Station, BB4 6DD
Ramsbottom Station, BL0 9AL
www.eastlancsrailway.org.uk
Tel: 01617 647790

Ecclesbourne Valley Railway
Wicksworth, DE4 4FB
www.e-v-r.com
Tel: 01629 823076

Elsecar Heritage Railway
Elsecar Heritage Centre, S74
8HJ
www.elsecarrailway.co.uk
Tel: 01226 740203

Embsay & Bolton Abbey
Steam Railway
Bolton Abbey Station, Skipton,
BD23 6AF
www.
embsayboltonabbeyrailway.
org.uk
Tel: 01756 710614
Talking Timetable: 01756
795189

Epping-Ongar Railway
Ongar Town, CM5 9AB
www.eorailway.co.uk
Tel: 01277 365200

Foxfield Steam Railway
Blythe Bridge, ST11 9BG
www.foxfieldrailway.co.uk
Tel: 01782 396210

Gloucestershire Warwickshire
Railway
Toddington Station, GL54 5DT
Winchcombe Station, GL54
5LB
www.gwsr.com
Tel: 01242 621405

Great Central Railway
Loughborough Central Station,
LE11 1RW
Quorn & Woodhouse, LE12
8AW
Leicester North, LE4 3BR
www.gcrailway.co.uk_
Tel: 01509 632323

Gt Central – Nottingham
Ruddington, NG11 6JS
www.gcrn.co.uk
Tel: 0115 9405705

Gwili Railway
Carmarthen, SA33 6HT
www.gwili-railway.co.uk
Tel: 01267 230666

GWR (Steam Museum)
Swindon, SN2 2EY
www.steam-museum.org.uk
Tel: 01793 466646

Isle of Wight Steam Railway
Havenstreet, PO33 4DS
www.iwsteamrailway.co.uk
Tel: 01983 882204

Keighley & Worth Valley
Railway
Haworth Station, BD22 8NJ
Keighley Station, BD21 4HP
www.kwvr.co.uk
Tel: 01535 645214

Kent and East Sussex Railway
Tenterden Station, TN30 6HE
www.kesr.org.uk
Tel: 01580 765155
Talking Timetable: 01580
762943

Lakeside & Haverthwaite
Railway
Haverthwaite Station, LA12
8AL
www.lakesiderailway.co.uk
Tel: 01539 531594

Lavender Line
Isfield Station, TN22 5XB
www.lavender-line.co.uk
Tel: 01825 750515

Lincolnshire Wolds Railway
Ludborough, DN36 5SH
www.lincolnshirewoldsrailway.
co.uk
Tel: 01507 363881

Llangollen Railway
Llangollen Station, LL20 8SN
www.llangollen-railway.co.uk
Tel: 01978 860979

Mangapps Farm Railway
Museum
Burnham-on-Crouch, CM0
8QG
www.mangapps.co.uk
Tel: 01621 784898

Middleton Railway
Hunslet, LS10 2JQ
www.middletonrailway.org.uk
Tel: 0845 680 1758

Mid-Norfolk Railway
Dereham Station, NR19 1DF
www.mnr.org.uk
Tel: 01362 851723

Mid-Hants Railway
(Watercress Line)
Railway Station Alresford,
SO24 9JG
Ropley Station, SO24 0BL
www.watercressline.co.uk
Tel: 01962 733810

Midland Railway Centre
Butterley Station, DE5 3QZ
Swanwick Junction
www.midlandrailwaycentre.
co.uk
Tel: 01773 570140

Mid-Suffolk Light Railway
Wetheringsett, IP14 5PW
www.mslr.org.uk
Tel: 01449 766899

National Railway Museum
Leeman Road, York, YO26
4XL
www.nrm.org.uk
Tel: 08448 153139

Nene Valley Railway
Wansford Station, PE8 6LR
www.nvr.org.uk
Tel: 01780 784444

Northampton & Lamport
Railway
Pitsford & Brampton Station,
NN6 8BA
www.nlr.org.uk
Tel: 01604 820327

Northamptonshire Ironside
Railway Trust
Northampton, NN4 9UW
www.nirt.co.uk
Tel: 01604 702031

North Norfolk Railway
Sheringham Station, NR26
8RA
Holt Station, NR25 6AJ
www.nnrailway.co.uk
Tel; 01263 820800

North Tyneside Steam Railway
(Stephenson Railway Museum)
North Shields, NE29 8DX
www.twmuseums.org.uk

North York Moors Railway
Pickering, YO18 7AJ
Goathland, YO22 5NF
Grosmont, YO22 5QE
www.nymr.co.uk
Tel: 01751 472508

Pallot Steam, Motor & General
Museum
Jersey, C.I.
www.pallotmuseum.co.uk
Tel: 01534 865307

Peak Rail
Matlock, DE4 3NA
www.peakrail.co.uk
Tel: 01629 580381

Plym Valley Railway
Plympton, PL7 4NW
www.plymrail.co.uk

Pontypool & Blaenavon
Railway
Blaenavon, NP4 9ND
www.pontypool-and-
blaenavon.co.uk
Tel: 01495 792263

Railway Preservation Society
of Ireland
www.steamtrainsireland.com

Rutland Railway Museum
Cottesmore, LE15 7BX
www.rutnet.co.uk
Tel: 01572 813203

Severn Valley Railway
Bridgnorth, WV16 5DT
Bewdley, DY12 1BG
Kidderminster, DY10 1QX
www.svr.co.uk
Tel: 01299 403816

South Devon Railway
Buckfastleigh, TQ11 0DZ
www.southdevonrailway.co.uk
Tel: 0843 3571420

Southall Railway Centre
Southall, UB2 4SE
www.gwrpg.co.uk
Tel: 0208 574 1529

Spa Valley Railway
Tunbridge Wells, TN2 5QY
www.spavalleyrailway.co.uk
Tel: 01892 537715

Strathspey Railway
Aviemore, PH22 1PY

www.strathspeyrailway.co.uk
Tel: 01479 810725

Swanage Railway
Swanage, BH19 1HB
www.swanagerailway.co.uk
Tel: 01929 425800

Swindon & Crickslade Steam
Railway
Blunsdon, Wilts.
www.swindon-crickslade-
railway.org.uk
Tel: 01793 771615

Tanfield Railway
Gateshead, NE16 5ET
www.tanfield-railway.co.uk
0845 463 4938

Telford Steam Railway
Horsehay, TF4 2NG
www.telfordsteamrailway.
co.uk

West Somerset Railway
Minehead Station, TA24 5BG
Williton Station, TA4 4RQ
Bishops Lydeard, TA4 3RU
www.westsomersetrailway.
co.uk
Tel: 01643 704996